Also by Marge Piercy

Poetry
BREAKING CAMP
HARD LOVING
4-TELLING (with Bob Hershon, Emmett Jarrett and Dick Lourie)
TO BE OF USE
LIVING IN THE OPEN
THE TWELVE-SPOKED WHEEL FLASHING
THE MOON IS ALWAYS FEMALE
CIRCLES ON THE WATER: Selected Poems
STONE, PAPER, KNIFE
MY MOTHER'S BODY

Fiction
GOING DOWN FAST
DANCE THE EAGLE TO SLEEP
SMALL CHANGES
WOMAN ON THE EDGE OF TIME
THE HIGH COST OF LIVING
VIDA
BRAIDED LIVES
FLY AWAY HOME
GONE TO SOLDIERS

Play
THE LAST WHITE CLASS (with Ira Wood)

Essays
PARTI-COLORED BLOCKS FOR A QUILT

Anthology
EARLY RIPENING: American Women's Poetry Now

Available Light

AVAILABLE LIGHT

by Marge Piercy

ALFRED A. KNOPF   New York   1988

THIS IS A BORZOI BOOK
PUBLISHED BY ALFRED A. KNOPF, INC.

Library of Congress Cataloging-in-Publication Data
Piercy, Marge. Available light. I. Title.
PS3566.I4A94 1988   811'.54   87-40490
ISBN 0-394-56474-X
ISBN 0-394-75691-6 (pbk.)

Various poems in this collection originally appeared in the following
publications: *The American Voice, Aspect, Calapooya Collage, Croton
Review, Footwork, Images, Kalliope, Lips, Manhattan Poetry Review,
The Massachusetts Review, Negative Capability, New Letters, New
Menorah, New Traditions, Open Places, Poets On, Sojourner, South
Coast Poetry Journal, The Southern California Anthology, Tendril,
Tikkun, Woman of Power,* and *Yellow Silk.*
"The last day of exile winds upward," "Love like a ticking bomb,"
and "Daughter of the African evolution" were originally published
in *Cotton Boll/Atlanta Review.*
"Eat fruit" and "Arles, 7 p.m." originally appeared in *Light Year '86*
and *Light Year '87*, published by Bits Press.
"Something to look forward to" originally appeared in *Women and
Aging: An Anthology by Women*, published by Calyx Books, 1986.

Manufactured in the United States of America

FIRST EDITION

Contents

JOY ROAD AND LIVERNOIS

Available light

Ripe and runny as perfect Brie, at this age
appetites mature rampant and allowed.
I am wet as a salt marsh under the flood tide
of the full solstice moon and dry as salt itself
that draws the superfluous juice from the tissues
to leave the desiccated butterfly wing intact.

I know myself as I know the four miles I walk
every morning, the sky like ice formed on skim
milk, the sky dappled and fat and rolling, never
the same two hours later. I know there are rooms
upon caverns opening off corridors I will never
enter, as well as those I'll be thrust into.

I am six with my mother watching Clippers
take off for Lisbon. I am nine and the President
whose voice is a personal god is dying in the radio.
I am twelve and coming while I mutter yes, yes,
of course, this is what the bones grow around to hold.
I am twenty-four as my best friend bleeds her life out.

At any moment I find myself under the water of my
past trying to breathe in that thick refracted medium.
At any moment a new voice is speaking me like a p.a.
system that one day amplifies a lecture on newts
and the next day jazz. I am always finding new
beings in me like otters swimming in the soup.

I have friends who gave themselves to Marx, to Freud,
to A.A., to Christianity or Buddhism or Goddess

3

religions, to the Party or the Lord or the Lover.
As a Jew, I have a god who returns me to myself
uncleaned, to be used again, since forgiveness must
be made but changes not one needle falling from the pine.

As consequences show their lengthened teeth
from the receding gums, we hunger for the larger
picture, the longer view, and yet and yet
I cannot augment the natural curve of earth
except by including the moth and the mammoth,
the dark river percolating through the sea

built rock, the dense memories of shell
and sediment, the million deaths recorded
in each inch; the warm funky breath
of Leviathan as he breached off the portside;
people in boots struggling to shove the pilot
whales free that a storm surge grounded.

In winter the light is red and short.
The sun hangs its wizened rosehip in the oaks.
By midafternoon night is folding in.
The ground is locked against us like a door.
Yet faces shine so the eyes stretch for them
and tracks in the snow are etched, calligraphy

I learn by rote and observation, patient
the way I am finally learning Hebrew
at fifty, forgiving my dead parents

who saw squinting by their own scanty light.
By four o'clock I must give up the woods,
come in, turn on every lamp to read.

Later when the moon has set I go out
and let the spears of Sirius and Rigel
pierce the ivory of my skull and enter
my blood like glowing isotopes of distance.
As I stand in the cold vault of the night
I see more and fainter stars as my eyes

clear or my blood cools. The barred owl
hoots. The skunk prances past me to stir
the compost pile with her sharp nails.
A lithe weasel flicks across the cul-de-sac.
Even the dead of winter: it seethes with more
than I can ever live to name and speak.

Joy Road and Livernois

My name was Pat. We used to read Poe in bed
till we heard blood dripping in the closet.
I fell in love with a woman who could ring
all bells of my bones tolling, jangling.
But she in her cape and her Caddy
had to shine in the eyes of the other pimps,
a man among monkeys, so she turned me on the streets
to strut my meek ass. To quiet my wailing
she taught me to slip the fire in my arm,
the white thunder rolling over till nothing
hurt but coming down. One day I didn't.
I was fifteen. My face gleamed in the casket.

My name was Evie. We used to shoplift,
my giggling, wide-eyed questions, your fast hands;
we picked up boys together on the corners.
The cops busted me for stealing, milled me,
sent me up for prostitution because I weren't
no virgin. I met my boyfriend in the courts.
Together we robbed a liquor store that wouldn't
sell us whiskey. I liked to tote a gun.
It was the cleanest thing I ever held.
It was the only power I ever had.
I could look any creep straight on in the eyes.
A state trooper blew my face off in Marquette.

My name was Peggy. Across the street from the gas-
works, my mom raised nine kids. My brother-
in-law porked me while my sister gave birth
choking me with the pillow when I screamed.
I got used to it. My third boyfriend knocked me up.

Now I've been pregnant for twenty years,
always a belly bigger than me to push around
like an overloaded wheelbarrow ready to spill
on the blacktop. Now it's my last one,
a tumor big as a baby when they found it.
When I look in the mirror I see my mom.
Remember how we braided each other's hair,
mine red, yours black. Now I'm bald
as an egg and nearly boiled through.

I was Teresa. I used to carry a long clasp
knife I stole from my uncle. Running nights
through the twitching streets, I'd finger it.
It made me feel as mean as any man.
My boyfriend worked on cars until they flew.
All those hot nights riding around and around
when we had noplace to go but back.
Those hot nights we raced out on the highway
faster faster till the blood fizzed in my throat
like shaken soda. It shot in an arc
when he hit the pole and I went out the windshield,
the knife I showed you how to use, still
on its leather thong between my breasts
where it didn't save me from being cut in two.

I was Gladys. Like you, I stayed in school.
I did not lay down in back seats with boys.
I became a nurse, married, had three sons.
My ankles swelled. I worked the night hours
among the dying and accident cases. My husband
left me for a girl he met in a bar, left debts,

a five-year-old Chevy, a mortgage.
My oldest came home in a body bag. My youngest
ran off. The middle one drinks beer and watches
the soaps since the Kelsey-Hayes plant closed.
Then my boy began to call me from the alley.
Every night he was out there calling, Mama,
help me! It hurts, Mama! Take me home.
This is the locked ward and the drugs
eat out my head like busy worms.

With each of them I lay down, my twelve-
year-old scrawny tough body like weathered
wood pressed to their pain, and we taught
each other love and pleasure and ourselves.
We invented the places, the sounds, the smells,
the little names. At twelve I was violent
in love, a fiery rat, a whip snake,
a starving weasel, all teeth and speed
except for the sore fruit of my new breasts
pushing out. What did I learn? To value
my pleasure and how little the love of women
can shield against the acid city rain.

You surge among my many ghosts. I never think
I got out because I was smart, brave, hard-
working, attractive. Evie was brave.
Gladys and Teresa were smart. Peggy worked
sixteen hours. Pat gleamed like olivewood
polished to a burnish as if fire lived in wood.
I wriggled through an opening left just big enough
for one. There is no virtue in survival

8

only luck, and a streak of indifference
that I could take off and keep going.

I got out of those Detroit blocks where the air
eats stone and melts flesh, where jobs
dangle and you jump and jump, where there are
more drugs than books, more ways to die
than ways to live, because I ran fast,
ran hard, and never stopped looking back.
It is not looking back that turned me
to salt, no, I taste my salt from the mines
under Detroit, the salt of our common juices.
Girls who lacked everything except trouble,
contempt and rough times, girls
used like urinals, you are the salt
keeps me from rotting as the years swell.
I am the fast train you are traveling in
to a world of a different color, and the love
we cupped so clumsily in our hands to catch
rages and drives onward, an engine of light.

Hard time

A diamond is forever, diamond hard,
a chip of time, cutting glass
as pain cuts flesh. A diamond
is a petrified tear, sorrow
hardened by fierce sustained
pressure into something that
can stab, can endure, can break
but only if a flaw is found.

A diamond is coal that has suffered
and burned and crystallized
into a thing that takes light
into itself. Do you know
where diamonds come from?
Whose suffering is this you wear
glinting at your ear, winking
from your finger? How many
children's eyes shine in it?

There is something once soft
that grows hard, bright
as the pressure crushes it.
There is something once soft
that burns harder than steel
in the furnace of pain.

Call it a diamond. Call it
the heart of a people.
Call it the heart of pain
crystallized to something that
can gouge armor, something
that stands in the ashes
of the terrible fire.

Nothing is forever, not
prison, not the pain
of a people pressed down,
not the eyes of children shining
and then dimmed, not
diamonds glinting like
chips of frozen sun.
This is not a jewel
I would wear lightly.
This is not a jewel
I would wear.

Daughter of the
African evolution

The beauty of the great predators amazes me,
the music of their sleek haunch muscles rippling,
the clear fierce gaze with the fire of hunger
dancing golden in those slitting pupils,
the way the hawk plays in the columns of air,
the snow leopard balances leaps with her heavy
tail among the rocks. I have made friends
with a couple in captivity, as slow
as the shadow of a tree moves across the grass.

The grace of the fast grazers dazzles me,
the gazelle tossing her neck, streaking
so her hooves seem to float over the ground,
the stylish avant-garde striping of the zebra
gorgeous and improbable, a parade except against
their proper sun/shade pattern, vanishing
into camouflage; the storm cloud glory of the horse,
the antelope the color of velvet dust,
the calm guilt-provoking gaze of ruminants.

But I am neither. I honor my mothers,
the scuttling mammals hustling through the brush
who gobbled through life, a little of this,
a little of that, a lot of what others left,
grasshoppers, a nice fat mouse, raspberries
in season, rotten apples to get drunk on,

roots we dug for, never efficiently. Not
specialized to do anything particularly well
except try to stay out of trouble and survive.

Those middling animals, the small predators
like the feral cat always chasing dinner
and scrambling away from being eaten; the small
grey fox who picks grapes on the high dunes
and will steal a melon or a goose. Behold
my ancestral portraits: shambling field
apes smallish and chattering, with babies
hanging on their backs picking over the fruit
like my grandmother, my mother and like me.

Eat fruit

Keep your legs crossed, Mother said. Drinking
leads to babies. Don't hang around street corners.
I rushed to gulp moonshine on corners, hip outthrust.
So why in the butter of my brain does one marble tablet
shine bearing my mother's commandment, eat fruit?

Here I stand, the only poet from whom
you can confidently obtain after a reading
enough mushy tan bananas to bake bread
should you happen to feel the urge at ten
some night in East Lansing or Boise.

You understand how needful it is, you say,
that I should carry the products of Cape
Cod such as oranges and kiwis with me
because surely they sell none in Seattle.
Suppose South America should be blockaded?

Others litter ash, beer cans. I leak pits.
As we descend into Halifax while my seat partner
is snorting the last of his coke, I am the one
choking as I gobble three apples in five minutes,
agricultural contraband seized at borders.

Customs agents throw open my suitcase and draw
out with gingerly leer from under my negligee
a melon. Drug smugglers feed their self-importance,
but me they hate along with the guy trying to smuggle
in a salami from the old country his uncle gave him.

I am the slob who makes gory stains on railroad seats
with fermenting strawberries. You can recognize me
by the happy cloud of winged creatures following my head.
I have raised more fruitflies than genetics labs.
I have endowed ant orphanages and retirement communities.

However, I tell you smugly, I am regular in Nome,
in Paducah, in both Portlands and all Springfields.
While you are eating McMuffins I am savoring a bruised
but extremely sophisticated pear that has seen five
airports and four cities and grown old in wisdom.

I see the sign and tremble

I first saw that sign off the MidCape highway and thought
I dreamed it in two a.m. fatigue bleary as drunkenness;
then in a dying city on a rusty steamer table
of street, there it was offering
convenience, preservation and power at once:
Self Storage.
                    Who would have guessed it?
I could have salted them all away, safely out
of my sight: the gang girl running over the tarred
roofs sticky under her sneakers; the existentialist
in black turtleneck and black jeans with hair
ironed straight down her back and a butt pasted
to her lower maroon painted lip; the French hausfrau
trying, trying to do it the right bourgeois way;
the eager scholar in the stacks over Lake Michigan
wrestling with Wordsworth as an irritable moose;
the madwoman charging the police barricades, on fire
with an indignation gone nova and threatening
to burn her to a black hole of despair;
the New York femme fatale dancing through a maze of mirrors
built of six lovers, reflecting all faces but hers,
juggling her hours like glass bowls of hot coffee;
the greatlapped mama dispensing tisanes
and stew; the Marxist logic chopper brandishing
trendy quotes; the invalid dying of smoking and gas,
coughing blood while she lay with a great
steam press closing on her chest, and friends
and lovers fled from the presence of death

as if from a server of subpoenas; the wife
with two husbands trading jokes over her head
held responsible for moonshine, weather, onset
of local ice ages inside and out; the woman alone
in the Midwest of a rented room sent into exile
from her commune, sending back paychecks
and sucking loneliness like an icicle igniting
her teeth that never melted in any warmth
she could offer, and none was offered her;
the forty-four-year-old jumping without a chute
into love as into a fire and thriving;
the betrayer, the betrayed, the loyal friend,
the sore loser, the reluctant winner,
the ascetic reading de Sade in penance,
the gourmand, the pious Jew, the pagan.

Sometimes I find no self in me
but a hungry multitude demanding the use
of my body. Self-storage? Is that all
poems are?
                   We are four-fifths water
and when we die, what remains after the fluids
dry but a stain and the many colored grits
of the ashes, like a puzzle that won't assemble?

Not the wornout wardrobe of self, a knockdown **rummage**
sale of smelly lusts and stains of fear and meals
dribbled and holes burned for little stars of flesh

to sparkle through. Only what we did, what we made
and what we botched: that shines on
eventually through all the red shifts of distance,
the shape of the constellation our best
and worst acts finally reveal to others,
not to us, buffeted in the center of the explosion
we call our lives.

The fecund complain
they are not honored

To please a critic you should write little,
a book every ten years. That shows how hard
you work, slow as a glacier advancing,
and critics, who may wish to write
sometimes lying in bed in the morning,
can justify abstention. Ten years
of wild soul struggle, although we secretly
know better. We do what matters to us.

The driven work. They get up like Sylvia
long before dawn. They write in buses.
They write in the laundromat while clothes
flash by, and somebody steals their socks.
They write on computers if one is there;
if not, they write in pencil or crayon;
lacking paper, they scribble on matchbook covers
and menus. They use the palm of their hand.

The driven get ideas in the bathtub
and sit down still dripping and spoil
the chair. The driven get a great idea
at the worst moment, panting and heaving
and blow the orgasm or lose their erection
as the casing may be. They burn the beans,
disconnect the phone, are rude to callers,
and yet in the middle of the down-filled

night, the muse walks back and forth
across their belly in boots with cleats

cursing and kicking and singing the praises
of the unborn poems and the untold stories
till they swarm like fish babies nipping
the flanks of sleep. When the driven die
their real inner stone reads: you did
a little piece of it, a little piece.

Proximity fuses

The country is too much itself
to refract exact years, crossroad
of muskrat, mallard, heron, deer,
the societies of warblers in the high
intricate green tree worlds flittering.
Human dramas implode without trace.
But when I walk the lower east side or upper west side

of New York, when I climb the short hills under big
floppy oaks of Ann Arbor, coming up from the canal
in the Xe arrondissement, in the Mission,
whenever I cross Cambridge or Berkeley on foot,
suddenly I find myself awash in the past, as if a freak
storm had let loose a flash flood down a gulley.
I thrash drowning, ground among boulders in a muddy
        uproar of pain.

Standing becalmed on a corner of Avenue A among the
        junkies
and the yuppies, I wonder why a sacrificial stone knife
is turning in my liver until I stare carefully around.
Under those eaves he lay groaning. That was the storefront
where lovers stretched each other on the wheel of dogma
until every bone was prized from its socket.
That rowhouse is a bomb exploding each time I pass.

The white clapboard of that Victorian pile leaks radioactive
passion. I pass through a museum where icons of my past

stand still engaged under the fall of the ax,
are bound still singing in the fire.
If I climbed that narrow dim stairway
I would find myself impaled there on a flaming sword.
Innocence is just another word for pain.

I hurry on as if the past could trap me inside itself.
The fires of memory burn but do not consume. I fear
being caught, a hamster on a treadmill
running furiously in place till my heart bursts.
To remember is to relive under knowledge's white light.
My inferno enacts itself at any time
on dingy urban streets.

The Blah Blah Blues

A big floppy ragdoll child groping
for the breast, I straggle back to my hillside.
Too much talking of nonsense thins the blood
till it can't bear in its red trucks
the weight of oxygen to feed the brain.
I have blabbed myself into the walls of bland rooms.
Too many fluorescent lights have greyed my skin
like a corpse underwater for days.

Being photographed does evaporate the soul.
Too much time in jets at thirty-five thousand
feet where the radioactive spears penetrate
the spine and breasts causes the womb
to shrivel to a potato stored all winter.
My face came off on motel room towels.
My poems were written by an impostor: me.
If I turn my eyes inward, cold fog swirls.

I beg the cats to knead me into form, purring.
I beg the trees to lean over pouring
green endurance through me till my nails
unclench their frozen buds. Beg you
to pick up this waif clinging to a battered
spar of self-pity, whining only the waterlogged
language of complaint, pretend I am a person,
and love me back into my flesh.

The bottom line

That white withered angel cancer
steals into a house through cracks,
lurks in the foundation, the walls,
litters down its infinitesimal dandruff
from school ceilings into children's lungs.

That invisible fungus hides in processed food,
in the cereal, the salami, the cake.
Welcomed into the body like a friend
it proceeds to eat you from inside,
parasitic wasp in a tomato worm.

Out of what caprice quenched in a moment's
pleasure does the poison seep?
We come to mistrust the body
a slave to be starved to submission,
an other that can like a rabid dog

turn on and bite a separate me.
But the galloping horse of the thighs,
the giraffe of the spine are innocent
browsing their green. We die of decisions
made at three fifteen in boardrooms.

We die of the bottom line. We die
of stockholders' dividends and a big bonus
for top executives and more perks. Cancer
is the white radioactive shadow of profit
falling across, withering the dumb flesh.

Wrong Monday

First the alarm is mute. Forgot the plunger.
I discover the milk is sour right after
I pour it on cereal. I pad
to the door stepping into what the cat
threw up. I clean the floor and then
my hands smell bad. Washing them
I splash my blouse and have to change.
After driving for an hour I remember
I forgot to pack underwear and the speech
I'm paid to give. The next sign
I see is ROAD CONSTRUCTION
NEXT 144 MILES. At that moment
stalled in traffic, my period starts.

Something to look forward to

Menopause—word used as an insult:
a menopausal woman, mind or poem
as if not to leak regularly or on the caprice
of the moon, the collision of egg and sperm,
were the curse we first learned to call that blood.

I have twisted myself to praise that bright splash.
When my womb opens its lips on the full
or dark of the moon, that connection
aligns me as it does the sea. I quiver,
a compass needle thrilling with magnetism.

Yet for every celebration there's the time
it starts on a jet with the seatbelt sign on.
Consider the trail of red amoebae
crawling onto hostess' sheets to signal
my body's disregard of calendar, clock.

How often halfway up the side of a mountain,
during a demonstration with the tactical police
force drawn up in tanks between me and a toilet;
during an endless wind machine panel with four males
I the token woman and they with iron bladders,

I have felt that wetness and wanted to strangle
my womb like a mouse. Sometimes it feels cosmic
and sometimes it feels like mud. Yes, I have prayed
to my blood on my knees in toilet stalls
simply to show its rainbow of deliverance.

My friend Penny at twelve, being handed a napkin
the size of an ironing board cover, cried out
Do I have to do this from now till I die?
No, said her mother, it stops in middle age.
Good, said Penny, there's something to look forward to.

Today supine, groaning with demon crab claws
gouging my belly, I tell you I will secretly dance
and pour out a cup of wine on the earth
when time stops that leak permanently;
I will burn my last tampons as votive candles.

Loving the crone

Two sisters, seventy and seventy-two, jogging
one morning, are followed two blocks
by a carload of boys hooting and mocking
because they found it ludicrous
that women should age and yet live.

Two useful lives, union organizers,
lovers and friends abounding, still avid
to argue the day's paper at breakfast.
The picket lines they marched in
would parade from iced pole to pole.

Almost everyone sitting before me imagines
if you are clever, if you exercise to pain,
follow fashion, consume the right products,
you will never get old. Fourteen forever!
The ultimate ambition of our time.

Rich old men run the world, crunching the pliant
bones of teenagers for celery hors d'oeuvres.
Children are broken on the rampant pricks
of men who hate women. The ultimate desire:
a child who can't reach orgasm.

Consequence exists like the bones in your hand.
One used woman: we are hourly told
that living makes us stupid. The more
we have done, the less we have to say.
Old woman, hag, bag, crone, witch:

in contempt for the mother's body it begins.
In blood it ends. If use makes us less,
then we long to be androids, perfect
as convertibles in the showroom, programmed
to satisfy everyone but ourselves.

If living makes women crazy, then living
is crazy. We are throwing away too much,
family heirlooms lining the westward trail.
Whenever we weep, if we understand
we may grow like a stalactite longer, stronger.

If we do not honor wisdom, we are doomed
to stupidity, pea brains in our dinosaur tails
ready to run ten miles around and around,
a gerbil in a cage, or a blinded
workhorse turning some owner's mill.

Dog Street number

Growling through the glass
from the second floor kitchen
window slantwise down
at the doberman across the street
Jim Beam looks mean
as a rusty nail sticking
up from a plank, hot
nasty as a grease fire
smoking up the kitchen,
tough as a blackjack.

He sneers against the glass,
his fur wrinkling,
mahogany motorcycle jacket
eyes slitted, shining.
If I could get at you.
Oh yeah? If the glass
broke, it would be the dog
leaping hot at you,
your small bones
crunching in his teeth.

You bring to mind girls
on streetcorners strutting
hair frizzed, straightened, blown
in the latest bad girl style,
skirts too short, too long,

too tight, too baggy
depending on what shocks
teachers and the world
of chalk water boredom
they stand for that year.

They too say, fuck you,
world, show me
what you got, honey,
I'm tough, I'm ready,
and the world smiles
thinly, wetly,
a hungry tiger crouching
belly low to begin
a sensuous creep
toward fresh food.

Down the road,
down the road

My younger self fled not toward but from:
out of the steel rim horizon of the Middle West
that never moves, the converging metal compass legs
of the railroad tracks, the highway that heat
shimmers over wriggling through a shallow
lake of boiling asphalt, driving flat out
or more often carried away on somebody
else's wheels.
                          I was born near the tracks.
Soon I was waving at brakemen till they threw
fat thumbs of chalk. With them we scrawled fuck
on walls or drew hopscotch patterns on sidewalks
with equal zest. I gloated on boxcars passing,
Erie Lackawanna, Chesapeake and Ohio, Southern
Pacific, Santa Fe, Great Northern, stations
of paradise. Our house was arcanely marked
that hoboes could get a handout, for my mother
never forgot the sour taste of hunger. I yearned
for those trains, never guessing our line was
the Detroit Terminal Railroad, going noplace
but round the city in circles, through
the west side ghetto to the east side ghetto.

In college I would set out for New York with anyone,
would pile in for Chicago with a toothbrush and
panties in my purse. Wherever I was was inferior
to where I might be. Simply moving on was proof
I was getting someplace, and someplace else

was sufficient goal to prod my butt aloft.
Names on maps were powers I must possess.

Now I am yearning home, driven as a pigeon
that must align its stubby body with the magnetic
field that feels just right. I am paranoid
about swirls of snow, blizzards building walls
of weather to stymie my eastward flight.
Home, I am muttering, home, home, home, home
maddened as a migrating herd, all hooves and antlers
and temper and need, not willing to loiter,
not willing to turn my head right or left
but bulling on raspy dry with thirst for just
the water that flows from my own well, weary
for just my own bed under my own crazy quilt,
wanting to waken to just the birds I feed
calling from my own marsh and woods my name.

SLIDES

Slides from our recent European trip

1. Avebury

In Kennet Avenue among the monoliths
not stolen or knocked down, sheep are grazing.
They glance at us, then turn downcast away.
Sheepish, Woody cries, joyful with etymology.
And they follow each other just like sheep!

Sometimes language bears in its fossil rock
things once commonly known, now information
available to us only as tourists
like the sheepishness of sheep,
the balls in testify, as here poke through the earth,
through the welter of houses from the last thousand years,
through country roads, prim churches, blowzy pubs,
those male and female stones, the huge breast
called Silbury Hill, vast and cumbersome
works of a people whose will slumbers
in the stone circles, rows, wordless
as the thoughts of the sheep that sniff us.

Yet that will is potent, not with the dumb ferocity
and shapeliness of mountains, not with the bodily
eloquence of frightened or curious sheep.
Here are erected runes of language partly designed
to be read by clouds or goddesses, left for us
too carefully wrought to be ignored.
Sometimes with my hands on the warm/cold stone
I almost think I hear it in my bones.

2. Dartmoor

Under the sky, in the sky almost, the sky arching down
sometimes descending as fog thick as still water
compressing sounds and blotting out paths,
dissolving directions, I wander, wander
a little drunk always with the air my lungs
bubble to as my mouth would take champagne.

A person is tall here. A sheep is tall.
A standing stone looms visible for miles.
This is not Israel, not Russia or even Wales,
not a land my ancestors left their bones in,
bled on, escaped to or from.
                              Yet I come home here.
I dream from something deep under my feet.

Each visit the hunger starts and my feet draw me
as if I were iron to a magnet hidden one hill
further onward. I never bring a camera onto the moors.
Their vast flat lines and long slow curves
defy boxed images. You have to dance
to their long music, turn and trot and turn again.

Their beauty is of scale and somber hues,
the heather and bracken tones, the sullen lurid
green of bogs with toothy sticky mouthed plants,
the ponies scenting us and tossing scrubby

manes and trotting off. Both sheep and stones
the same clean light weathered grey.

The stones draw me from the center of my body.
I rub against them the way the sheep do, tufts
of wool strewn at their base like offerings.
They make me want to fuck slowly and for hours.
The tors are wrinkled rock expressive and fierce.
From any of them you can watch the sky change the land.

Any good dowser can tell you that land not over
violated and over built, not gouged at, poisoned,
can bow cello chords from the spine to its inner
music. I am a dowser of images. Over this earth
my breastbone dips and shimmies like hazel
crying what rises here to slake deep thirst.

3. Dead Waters

At Aigues Mortes the dog was a practiced beggar.
He patrolled not the big lot where buses disgorge
but a small seaward lot near the private quarter.

We ate our picnic lunch, gazing at the ramparts.
He honed his longing stare on us till we tossed
bits of sausage he caught deftly and bolted.

Finally we threw him a baguette, whole and slightly

stale, thinking he would leave it, teasing him.
But his ears rose as if he heard a fine clear

high note our ears could not reach. He caught the loaf.
He laid it down to examine and then he seized it,
tossed his head smartly and set off at a rapid trot,

the prized baguette in his teeth. Other picnickers called
to him, we tossed after him a bit of sausage, but
he could not be lured back. Off he went in a straight

line at the ramparts and then all along them
to the far gate when he headed in and ran home,
never pausing under the white fish eye of the steamed sun.

A whole loaf of bread. What did that mean to him?
The thing humans never give him? Therefore precious?
Or simply something entire, seamless, perfect for once.

4. The housing project at Drancy

Trains without signs flee through Paris.
Wrong trains. The wrong station.
The world as microwave oven, burning from within.
We arrive. Drancy looks like Inkster,
Gary, the farther reaches of Newark.

In the station they won't give directions.
C'est pas notre affaire. We don't deal with that.
Outside five buses limp in five directions

into the hot plain drugged with exhaust.
Nobody ever heard of the camp. They turn away.

Out on the bridge, over marshaling yards:
Here Jews were stuffed into cars nailed shut.
Here children too young to know their names
were counted like so many shoes
as they begged the French police hemming them in

Take me to the bathroom, please, please,
before I wet myself. Mother, I have been so good,
and it is so very dark. Dear concierge,
I am writing to you as everyone else
is dead now and they are taking me away.

Yes, to the land children named Pitchepois,
giant's skull land grimmer than Hansel came to.
On the bridge I saw an old bald workman
staring down and I told myself desperately,
He is a communist and will answer me.

I asked him where the camp was, now a housing
project. He asked, Why do you want to know?
I had that one ready. No talk of novels, research.
My aunt was there. Oh, in that case,
he pointed to distant towers. You want that bus.

Where we descended the bus, Never heard of it.
Eyes that won't look. Then a woman asked that
same question, Why do you want to know?

A housing project crammed with mothers.
The guard towers are torn down and lindens grow.

In flats now with heat and plumbing, not eighty
but one family lives. Pain still rises,
the groaning of machinery deep underfoot.
Crimes ignored sink into the soil like PCBs
and enter the bones of children.

5. Font-de-Gaume

Unbirthed. With only the flickering
torches licking at the hairy flanks
of the dark, she forced her way in,
through the cervix of the earth,
up the wet rock of the birth canal
into the chamber of the mother.

The terror gave her power.
I have a womb too, she would whisper,
the dark pressing on her face
like a mad lover, in the cold
always March in the earth, the time
ice melts and the green shoots poke.

The animals are female, male
carefully drawn, tender, roused,

ready to flee. We no longer know
the intimacy with prey that made
her man kneel to the deer
as he prepared to kill it for food.

Down deep in the mother's cold womb
she bargained for life and death,
for herds drumming their heels
on the ground, for fat sleek
mothers giving birth in the spring,
for males bellowing challenge in the fall.

Her line was not coarser
because her shapes conjured food.
When the sacred is sexual and the sexual
sacred, in all joining
some bird watches perched
and the earth is pleasured too.

6. Arles, 7 p.m.

Shoals of Americans scout supper,
flashing silver speed darting in the sidestreets,
faces green with low blood sugar,
follow the leader through squares lined with restaurants
all closed, all locked.
A busboy sweeping the sidewalk is sighted,

surrounded like a foreign correspondent
back from the front.
When, oh when do you open?

At eight o'clock finally seated
I am waiting for supper.
At eight-thirty the menu makes its appearance,
long contemplated outside, memorized,
the seventy-franc special drooled on, but
no the proper moment has not come
to take the order, for the moment
of order-taking must ripen like cheese
put away to mold in mountain caves.

At nine o'clock the order is taken,
waiting, waiting for supper.
At nine-fifteen the waiter returns.
Tonight there is no John Dory,
John Dory gone down with all hands lost.
Anything else, a fried mouse, please!
roast plucked tourist under glass,
stewed gendarme on blanched greenbacks
while waiting, waiting for supper.

The waiter looks delicious with
his sleeves slightly rolled.
He flees past our table, but I am
eying a chihuahua. If I had
a tidbit to entice him
I'd eat it, and him.

This napkin is a little starchy
but goes down with salt,
waiting, waiting for supper.

At nine-thirty the bread comes.
At nine-thirty-five it is all eaten.
Waiting, waiting for supper.
At ten o'clock the soup arrives,
the basic Mediterranean fish soup
I make myself in half the time I have
been sitting here and I drink it
slurp slurp and it is gone.
Waiting, waiting for supper.

At half past ten the lamb arrives
and at ten-thirty-five I crunch the last bone,
the potatoes, the salad, vanished
into the maw of a hunger that
could yawn and devour Arles, I
Kali, Gargantua, Godzilla
on a feeding frenzy biting
into domes crunch like spun sugar,
chewing stones and plaster, chomping trees.

If I ate your city, that
would teach you to leave me here
waiting, waiting for supper.
Ah, eleven. Food finally tucked in.
Now comes the bill.
Now comes the indigestion.

Travel is broadening. In a matter
of hours we start
waiting for breakfast.

7. Black Mountain

On Montagne Noire creeping everywhere under the beech
        trees
were immense black slugs the size and pattern
of blown truck tires exploded by the superhighway.
Diamonds patterned their glossy and glittering backs.

As we watched, leaves, whole flowers disappeared in three
        bites.
Such avidity rebuked our stomachs skittish with alien
water and strange food. In patches of sunlight filtered
down, the slugs shone like wet black glass.

Battlefields are like any other fields ; a forest
where men and women fought tanks with sten guns
houses as many owl and rabbit and deer as the next hill
where nothing's happened since the Romans passed by.

Yet I have come without hesitation through the maze
of lumbering roads to this spot where the small marker
tells us we have reached a destination. To die here
under hemlock's dark drooping boughs, better I think

than shoved into the showers of gas to croak like roaches
too packed in to flail in the intense slow pain
as the minutes like lava cooling petrified the jammed
bodies into living rock, basalt pillars whose fingers

gouged grooves in cement. Yes, better to drop in the high
clean air and let your blood soak into the rich leaf mold.
Better to get off one good shot. Better to remember trains
derailed, turntables wrecked with plastique, raids

on the munitions dump. Better to die with a gun
in your hand you chose to pick up and had time to shoot.
Dying you pass out of choice. The others come, put up
a monument decorated with crosses, no mogen davids.

I come avid and omnivorous as the shining slugs.
I have eaten your history and made it myth;
among the tall trees of your pain my characters walk.
A saw whines in the valley. I say kaddish for you.

Blessed only is the act. The act of defiance,
the act of justice that fills the mouth with blood.
Blessed is the act of survival that saves the blood.
Blessed is the act of art that paints the blood

redder than real and quicker, that restores
the fallen tree to its height and birds. Memory
is the simplest form of prayer. Today you glow
like warm precious lumps of amber in my mind.

COUNTRY PLEASURES

Implications of one plus one

Sometimes we collide, tectonic plates merging,
continents shoving, crumpling down into the molten
veins of fire deep in the earth and raising
tons of rock into jagged crests of Sierra.

Sometimes your hands drift on me, milkweed's
airy silk, wingtip's feathery caresses,
our lips grazing, a drift of desires gathering
like fog over warm water, thickening to rain.

Sometimes we go to it heartily, digging,
burrowing, grunting, tossing up covers
like loose earth, nosing into the other's
flesh with hot nozzles and wallowing there.

Sometimes we are kids making out, silly
in the quilt, tickling the xylophone spine,
blowing wet jokes, loud as a whole
slumber party bouncing till the bed breaks.

I go round and round you sometimes, scouting,
blundering, seeking a way in, the high boxwood
maze I penetrate running lungs bursting
toward the fountain of green fire at the heart.

Sometimes you open wide as cathedral doors
and yank me inside. Sometimes you slither

into me like a snake into its burrow.
Sometimes you march in with a brass band.

Ten years of fitting our bodies together
and still they sing wild songs in new keys.
It is more and less than love: timing,
chemistry, magic and will and luck.

One plus one equal one, unknowable except
in the moment, not convertible into words,
not explicable or philosophically interesting.
But it is. And it is. And it is. Amen.

A low perspective

Snow blink: that's light
hitting the bottomside of clouds,
when the earth shines secretly
like the moon, when white
fields glare at the sky.

In winter the late light
reddens on the bay
from the small hidden sun.
The waters stain the puffball
clouds with rusty flames.

The angles surprise the eye.
The clouds look heavy,
smoky, lit from below.
A winter joy, beautiful
but ominous, like the flight

of the great horned owl
floating across the clearing
against the hunger moon,
like the cannonball reports of ice
freezing, thawing on the ponds,

the sharp encounter, the doe pawing
in the yard, fox in the path,

bluejay waking me by rapping
his beak on the glass, irate
diner summoning the slow waiter,

feed us now or we starve.
A light thatching of snow:
every grass blade prickles.
This low light hardens the black
in every twig to precision.

Baboons in the perennial bed

Even after common sense whittles ambition
I always order too many seeds, bulbs, corms.
What's the lure? Why am I torn between
cutting the lily for my bedside and savoring
it daily on its pedestal of crisp leaves?

They rouse and sate the senses, touch,
sight, scent, the wild shagginess and precise
sculpted lines, the shadings of color from clang
to sigh. Yet I think what moves underneath
is pleased envy at their flagrancy.

They wave their sexual organs in the air,
the plants, colored far more freely than the hind-
quarters of baboons. We who are raised to shame
for the moist orchid between our thighs
must wish we were as certain of our beauty.

We don't have much
to say to each other

The redwing blackbirds have arrived in their hundreds,
a city of chirping, singing, peeping, chirring.
They are traffic, a convention. In the oaks and pines
they collect having loud conversations, a factory
of whistles. When somebody disturbs them, a cloud
stirs and then another and then another and another,
rising as if their row numbers had been called
to board the air in orderly sections. Yet
their noises suggest argument, excitement, at least
debate, and the males and females congregate
separate in their synagogue of tree, although
they are eying each other and posing.
They will pair and slip away soon, coming together
only to drive off the hawk, diving at his eyes.

When I come from the house and stand under their trees
they pay me no attention. I am neither a threat
nor a treat. They eat the food I have put down
without breaking their conversation. I am the casual
caterer of their business meeting. I am not dangerous
like a cat, a hawk, a man with a gun. My house
is only accidentally on their landing field,
and once they have scattered to their marshes,
they will rarely attend my feeders or my yard.
Once in a while canoeing I will come to them,
in the high maze of the Herring River, and the male
will be posted singing on a tall reed as I scull
past, his wings signaling to me, red, red,
and the nest and eggs will be hidden in the grass.

The answer to all problems

We aren't available, we can't talk to you
right now, but you can talk to us, we say,
but think of the astonishment if machines
suddenly spoke truth: What do you want?

You'd best have a damned good reason for bothering
me, intruding on my silence. If you're bored,
read a good book. Masturbate on your own time.
Call weather or your mother or a talk show.

If you're a creditor, I've just been cremated.
If you're my ex, I'm fucking a perfect body
in Acapulco. Hi, I'm too shy to answer.
I'm scared of obscene calls. I'm paranoid.

I'm sharing a bottle of wine and a loaf of bread
with my lover, our flesh smokes with desire,
our lips brush, our clothes uncoil hissing,
and you have a problem? Try prayer.

Hi obtuse one, it may be eleven on the West Coast
but it's two a.m. here and as you listen
a pitch too high for you to hear is giving
you herpes and melting your elastic and velcro.

Hi, this is the machine. My person is standing
two feet away to see if you're worth the effort.

Hi. If you hang up without leaving a message
your teeth will loosen overnight. I hate drones.

Hi, can my machine call your machine
and make an appointment? Can my machine
mate with yours and breed Walkmans?
Hi, my humans have been murdered and cannot come.

Open to the sky

It's a different sky every half hour all day:
Mouse grey clouds curdle. A high marbleized
overcast mimics the ruffled feathers of the bay.
Chicory blue and a dusting of white down.

They all have names: altocumulus undulatus,
cumulus congestus or fractus, cirrostratus,
names in Latin that never quite match
all that magnificent high hustle and heaping

of billows, that vast business colliding
miles up where the largest plane is tossed
and batted like a shuttlecock. The ocean
of air rages with its own bright storm.

Down here the oaks dash like inside out
umbrellas, the pines moan, the seagulls
shriek low and things torn loose crash
into the house. Wind flapping my hair

like a black wool shawl unraveling
I stand in the running squash vines
a battered scarecrow and the wind rushes
through me. Doors bang open and slam.

Great wind excites me as much as a lover.
In youth I was a slave to my moods;

now I am a creature of the weather, opening,
closing petals and apertures, quickened

to fizzing and seething, slowed
and thickened, sent spinning, clattering.
At fifty, the sun, the moon, the tides,
the seasons rule me like a field gone wild.

Love like a ticking bomb

The text was a discussion of his business problems.
The subtext was you. Always just on the edge
of my vision like a mote formed of opal and shadow
you were there, moving just out of range.

I was a pot on high simmer, dangerously
close to boiling and then bubbling over
with a stench of beef stew burning.
No lid could contain my scalding heat.

I was pregnant with the thought of you,
my body curling and coiling around you
and daily you grew in me bigger and bigger
till my organs were crushed by that heavy desire.

I went visiting, I ate meals, I sat
in front of television and movie screens
eyes glazed over like ponds just freezing opaque.
You were the hidden meaning of whatever I said.

Driving down the highway to Boston,
two figures in the front seat eyes forward
and between them, you sat, invisible:
the real drama was what you asked and I gave.

You were my daily addiction like cocaine,
a bottle of sherry in a drawer, the marathon

runner's high : you were the sweet secret vice
my life was organized around as a walled maze.

Inside that cocoon of wan dry passivity,
irrevocable change split that old life
open and out crawled a new avid creature
fully sexual on painted wings ready

to fly and mate at last. Sometimes
we get just what we want, and it alters
us ever after, neither better nor worse
but clearer, with different blood and face.

It doesn't suffice

Washing socks in the marble basin
that won't hold water, in a rehab
looking down on somebody else's yard
and life, I see that my cold water soap
says, Un très peu suffit. Mediterranean
sunlight singes my arm, which darkens
as I smell heated rock, wild lavender.

Outside the sky is the tall Midwestern
featureless grey—a very high lid—
that feels unconnected with the big
aimless flakes circling between old
red brick walls, thatching the spiky
weeds on a scorched rubble field
among coffin-narrow slum houses.

Not postcards, not vases or souvenirs
but homely objects conjure best for me,
pale pink thread—inside of white rabbit's ears—
I bought in a drygoods store in Mykonos
where a daisy-woman worked a loom singing.
As I sat on the bench, she guided me shoving
the woof as it shot through the bright wool.

I open the tin of my own herb tea, and from
the scent, the texture of monarda, thyme,
the rose petals still with the ghost of their
color, the borage, lovage, the sage,

fuzzy nubs of pineapple mint, darker spearmint,
catnip, lemon balm and sweet cicely leap up
the stone walks, the fruit of my summer garden.

In the cup, the earth of that hill of pines
rises in steam to taunt sinuses swollen
with dirty air. I taste the faint salt
of the long wind sweeping across the tawny
winter marsh still bleaching to wheatstraw.
The huge stars of home wheel in the cup of my
skull, dry for a taste of my well's water.

A penetrating cold

Insidious as fine rain
drizzle that seems more a state of mind
than an act of the atmosphere;

flattening as the mica schist northern
light that seeps in the high windows
throwing no shadows from the bare branches

outside, naked of leaf or bird or even
torn kite or lichen, ornamented only
by droplets slowly engorging;

meaningless as the dog chained across
the narrow lane among the builder's stash
of lumber, buckets, tools, ladders,

who barks all night at every car, cat,
broken bottle, until all the dogs on all
the hills give back ragged answers;

my emptiness curls round itself wishing
to sleep through the winter of your absence.
I am testy in my hunger, bearish, sullen.

Slowly my inner temperature sags and my
hair and nails slack their growth. My voice
if I used it would crack a skin of ice.

I tend my missing, a cranky egg-shaped cactus,
a plant lovely to no one. But on your return
it will bloom and bear fruit in one night.

The last day of
exile winds upward

I turn and turn around again, revolving
like an old woman who has dropped
something in the street, like a cat
that can't get comfortable, disliking
the smell on the blanket or hearth.

Here in these bleak rooms we camped two
months while time clotted, sour milk,
while time froze down to the bottom
mud and the quick fish perished in ice.
We survived in that frozen silt clutching.

Now I am back here with the northern light
grey as the eyes of dead fish glazed over
and suddenly I hear your voice in the next
room, and answer, fooled by the wish.
The silence sticks like burrs in my hair.

Anxiety bats me from wall to wall,
a sense that this is outside my life
as a ball is thrown out of a game and lost.
I want to bounce back and resume play.
I want to steal home and win the game.

I am packing up the last remnants of exile,
giving away food, a kettle, books,
divesting myself to rise into the wind.
Exile is a vessel I must crack to escape,
an egg of fired clay containing me.

I am growing sharp lizard claws and beak
of a fledgling hawk. I am pecking
the brittle walls till they crack.
Now I am scrabbling at the stormy sky
slamming off its rocky benches of cloud.

The other travelers, they snooze but I
am working hard, keeping this damned
rickety filthy plane up, ramming it forward.
My passion alone jets it through the storm
as the winds cast us loose dice finally

on the runway at Logan and we stumble out
even the flight attendants damp and scummy,
all of us green as early spring buds
bursting and I rush into your arms and we
speed through the night towards our bed.

The whole that is
made of wanting

Naked dancing among cacti and brambles,
barefoot over hot razor blades on skittish feet,
how often I threw myself to love
like a piece of meat dropped in a shark tank.

Trust is a flowering, fragrant, fragile.
Andante: the bud unclenches and the satin
of the peony opens with a languid rustle
till the trembling pollen is bared.

The doors of the spine swing on their squeaky
hinges. The belly opens its single eye to blink.
The hands loosen, water lilies on their pads.
The feet present themselves like hungry puppies.

Eat, drink, I am your daily bread
and you are mine made every morning fresh.
In the oven of the bed we rise and bake
yeasty, dark, full of raisins and seeds.

Rock on, my bed of trust feathered
with our hopes, a quilt worked of care
a patch at a time of all our old half-lives
velvet and burlap, denim and fur.

In a daily sunrise miracle we join our
dreams. When two open hands come together
they grasp, they hold on, and at last
they close on what they meant to find.

Dog days dogged rag

The crickets rub their legs so fast they zizz
so I imagine their thin dry legs sparking,
starting a fire, except that nothing would catch

on this concave day when every piece of paper
feels like overcooked linguini. Wood
of table, chair exudes a tacky grease.

This is not fire but only heat: life
in a slow pressure cooker. Steaming
preserves the vitamins. Yet no predators

bound after prey. They are all sleeping
under bushes, bellies to the still cool
earth the compress of leaves has saved.

Night comes as a clumsy lover pressing
you into clammy sheets; smothered
you gasp and loll, less a landed fish

than a drowning wombat who dreams
the thin dry air of mountaintops—not
its natural habitat, but is this steam table?

Surely I am cooked now. Turn me over,
sprinkle salt on me. Try me with garlic.
The other possibility is that god is a slug.

Reconciled

You have come back from your hike
up the sunblasted mountains of ego
and I have crawled out from my squat
in the wind caves of sulk.

We have argued, wept, fought
again, made love again.
At last we let silence flow in
like a long tide rising,

the full moon tide that seeps
into dry cracks in the rock;
that sweeps bladder wrack, skate
egg cases, the shells of moon

snails up to the base of the dunes;
that trickles into the tall beige grasses
who thought they grew from dry land;
that floats the wrecked dinghy upcreek.

Now it is afternoon at a party.
We dance two hundred feet up on the roof
of a millionaire's cottage.
Below, breakers crack their long

whips and fold over, foaming white
as clean sheets flapping taut.
Around us people drink, flirt.
I move my hips to you and to the waves,

thanking the sea that it has turned and risen.

Morning love song

I am filled with love like a melon
with seeds, I am ripe and dripping sweet juices.
If you knock gently on my belly
it will thrum ripe, ripe.

It is high green summer with the strawberries
just ending and the blueberries coloring,
with the roses tumbling like fat Persian
kittens, the gold horns of the squash blowing.

The day after a storm the leaves gleam.
The world is clear as a just washed picture window.
The air whips its fine silk through the hands.
Every last bird has an idea to insist on.

I am trying to work and instead
I drip love for you like a honeycomb.
I am devoid of fantasies clean as rainwater
waiting to flow all over your skin.

After the corn moon

Swallows thrown from a giant hand turn,
fleet motes, around each other hurtling
over the marsh and back. The young
grown, the flock assembles. On the wire
neat, formal, they turn sleek heads south.

Every rambling poison ivy vine burns
in a few scarlet leaves. Grass tawny
as lions, the salt meadow has fur now
rippling over bunched muscles in the wind,
leaner and raspier than last week,

hungrier for something to rub, something
to strip. The robins are drunk on rum
cherries. The garlic falls over, the rose
hips redden. Every day we peer at the grapes
watching them color, puckering sour.

The houses are all rented and the roads
jammed with people driving their tempers
flat out or boiling their brains dry
in traffic like percolators searing
good coffee to battery acid.

Soon they will go home and the ponds
will clean themselves of soapsuds and the piss
of psychiatrists' children and the fried clam
shacks will put up their shutters and the air
will smell of salt and pine again.

This land is a room where a party has gone
on too long. Nothing is left whole to break.
As the blowzy embrace of heat slackens
I long for the feisty bite of cold mornings,
the bracing smack of the sea wind after

the first storm, walking the great beach alone.
The bed of summer needs changing to roughened
sheets that smell of the line. Fall seeps in
like energy quickening till it bursts out
spurting crimson from creeper and tree.

Even in this heat I walk farther and faster
hearing the sea's rising mutter. The birds
seem all in a hurry. The season of death
and fruition comes near, of ripeness and rot.
Sometimes the knife of frost is a blessing.

In the dark all cats fly

Rising stars rush toward me.
I climb from the net of lights
into a darkness of panther fur.
I am focused now into the skies
bearing forward with locomotive lamp.

I fly like a cat gathering light
into my eyes. The city is cellophane
jewels below winking and flashing
but I soar into you, into you
till you surround me like black water.

How high we ride in darkness plumed
with amber streaks over the bay, turning
twin stars blazing round each other
till we fuse, and sparks litter down
seeking themselves in the white waves.

Nocturne

Raccoons on the roof clump and stomp
raucous on the asphalt, in volume
a dance party of bears overhead.

Waking suddenly blanketed in fog
I hear in the marsh a sharp cry
of a small bright life draining

in blood spurting out. A blundering
doe started crashes through thickets
nearer the house than she likes.

These sounds: skunks tripping on light feet
tossing the compost like salad.
The fox's dry cough, a match striking.

These: the whistling row of raccoons
mating, diesel locomotives in heat
leveling the bushes and snorting leaves.

I have seen the marten streak across the road.
I have watched mice dart on their trails
flashing through the dangerous square of light.

Suffering jet lag I lay one night in bed
and the great horned owl outside kept hooting
persistently as headache. I marveled

at the echo where none should be.
Higher pitched. Then I finally heard him
distinct, beating toward her. Her dark prince.

I grew up on sirens, a woman's cry repeated,
the payday drunken neighbor hurling his kids
out one by one to crash into our siding,

bottles tossed from cars to explode sparks
of broken glass in a moment's small fireworks,
cars bursting into speed side by side leaping.

When I first moved from the city, silence menaced
inert as too deep water pressing my chest;
now the night is populated again, familiar.

Silence on this world is only attention
unwhetted. Languages out of a night without neon
now slow and quicken my human blood.

Raisin pumpernickel

You shine, my love, like a sugar maple in October,
a golden-orange overarching blaze of leaves,
each painted its own tint of flames
tossed on the ground bright as silk scarves.
So are you happy.

My curly one, my stubborn fierce butter,
down with the head and charge all horns
and the blattering thunk of bone head on bone,
the smoke and hot rubber stench of overheated temper.
So are you angry.

The tomcat is a ready lover. He can do it at dawn
when the birds are still yawning, he can do it
while the houseguest walks up the drive, do it after
four parties and an all-night dance, on a convenient floor.
So are you able.

Your love comes down rich as the warm spring rain.
Now it charges like a tawny dark maned lion.
Now it envelopes me in wraiths of silken mist.
Now it is a thick hot soup that sustains me.
So are you loving.

You're an endless sink of love, a gaping maw
into which I shovel attention like soft coal
into an old furnace; you're a limitless love source,

a great underground spring surging out of rock
to feed a river.

You cry your needs, bold as a six-week kitten.
You're devious as a corporate takeover and direct
as an avalanche. What ten years into this conversation
commands my interest? You're still the best novel
I've ever read.

Secretly we both think we were bred for each other
as part of an experiment in getting dreams made
flesh and then having to feed on the daily bread
of passion. So we die and die with loving
and go on living.

La dolce far niente

I lack the gift for idleness,
to lie on the beach slowly roasting to the spine
while the hours like languid honeybees
crawl over my pollen-colored thighs.

My youth was when I did not own a watch.
Now my arm has a permanent pale circle.
Time issues its supercilious beeps,
but its rattling warning is pitched too high

to hear, vibrating the bones of my neck.
Work is my first joy and my last thought.
How sweet then is the thick poppy ooze
of idleness snatched like adultery

rare as a moonbow, the cozy waste
of puttering—the unnecessary tasks,
cataloguing, fiddling with drawers,
filing nails and yellowed letters,

poking through old intimacies, woolens
to which a scent of bergamot and sweat
cling. The hours gladly melt to a lump
of amber softening back to resin.

I do nothing best by doing small some-
things, a well fed butterfly flittering.
At such times even washing windows
has the odor of sin and bonbons.

Vegetable love

Outside gnarled rough black,
the shaggy radishes talk louder
and longer of earth than the red globes
or the white pricks; inside hot,
properly hot. I grew up
eating thin slices like rose windows
I would hold up to the light
then smear with schmaltz.
These black lumps keep in the earth
all winter; we pull them from straw
and snow to warm us.
Sometimes happy in bed I think
of black radishes, round, hefty,
full of juice and hot within,
just like our love.

Moon of the mother turtle

I am the busybody who interferes.
All through turtle mating season
I am hauling the females out of the road
and setting them where I presume
it is safe to lay their eggs.

Who appointed me guardian of turtles?
Yet when I see their bodies broken
like rotten pumpkins on the blacktop
I get so angry I have no choice but
to go on dragging them to sandbanks.

My least favorite duty is the two weeks
of snapping turtles. Occasionally I grasp
a weighty female and haul her out
of the way of cars before she can react.
Other times it's a wrestling match,

me with a stick and she with her beak,
neither of us prepared to back down,
a tug of war, wrestling, snarling
in the ruts of the old railroad right of way.
She must, she must. The eggs press

on her to be born. She is half mad.
Her eyes glitter dully as sun

glimpsed through muddy water. She is
the ancient of days raging with the urge
to dig and lay, dig and lay more.

I am a yelping dog circling, just as mad
to get her out of the roadway. She
hisses like a mother cat. Her great
beak clacks. She stinks like muck
from the basement of the fish maker's shop.

When finally I get her onto the bank, she
goes to it at once, sighing. A train
could pass two feet away as it used to
and she would lay on. I am forgotten
as I haul two ties to build her a rampart.

Then we go our separate ways, me toward
the bay to complete my four-mile walk,
she back to Bound Brook, dragging her
massive belly, each under our compulsions
like moons with the same and different faces.

A CANDLE IN A GLASS

Litter

I am always forgetting something.
The kettle boils dry and stinks.
The tiny green-shouldered tomato plants
while I'm writing a poem die of thirst
scorched under the glass of the hotbed.

I forget birthdays, I forget to call.
I forget the book I promised to bring.
I forget where I put my purse, my keys,
my wallet, my lenses, my love.
I lose my way in the night's black pocket.

I can't think of the name of the goddess
who stands at the gate blinking her one
great eye through the fog and the snarling
wind, sweeping her warning glance across
where the waves smash themselves kneeling.

I forget the way my mother laughed.
I forget her cake, the taste of the uncooked
dough, the just proportions of cinnamon and sugar.
I lose the touch of her fingers, stone
washed smooth by water and laid in the sun.

I lose the bread smell of my old cat's fur;
I lose the name and face of a man just out
of prison who crawled in my body to hide;

I lose the addresses of urgent people to whom
I promised much in towns I have forgotten.

What happened to my burnt orange shawl?
My bones are slowly dissolving in salt water.
It all falls away like feathers, like leaves,
like sand blowing. In the end I will say,
I was somebody maybe a woman I forget.

All the lost words and things and tasks
I have littered behind me are drifting on winds
round and up as if gravity had forgotten
to drop them, and sometimes in the night
I wake and the name comes to me and I shout

to the ceiling, Appomattox, rue de Sentier,
Emily Hannah, 8325 American Avenue,
metasomatism, two thirds to one,
and then lilacs, the scent of my mother's
white lilacs, thickens the air till I weep.

Edges of emptiness

Those who truly inhabit our lives
whose faces, whose gestures
like fine choreography align the air,
whose voices enter that ghostly inner ear
so that we shall hear them ten years
later in an empty room at dusk,
never can their presence be replaced.

Those with whom we are truly intimate
sometimes with hands and organs,
sometimes with the paste of words alone,
the creatures for whom the hollow
places of our solitude are opened wide
to shimmer with the lighted lamps of love,
we shape ourselves to hold them.

We have been configured to a use,
a habitation. We are the chambered
shell of a nautilus, the high steep
coil of a conch, and always those vaults,
those winding galleries of pearl
will futilely await the one whose need
and pleasure they hardened around.

In love we weave ourselves together,
Persian carpets with the colors
of each friendship knotted fine and tight,
the pattern as visible on the reverse.
That dance of hue and light we studied

to perfect will never again join.
Loneliness is general or precise:

broad as a wheatfield under a tall Nebraska
sky or narrow as a footpath between
cliff and canyon. Particular, we starve
at Thanksgiving table. Feed us voices, tales,
faces, ornaments, we suck a shard of glass.
Those hungers lodge in our bones where they
sign to the skilled in X-rays, until death.

For mourning

I wear grey for mourning, never black.
Black is my hair, black is the intense
night of the dark of the moon straight up,
the rarest wood and skin, the sleek of seals,
the shining of wide open pupils, the heart
of the poppy, the cat's patent leather flank.

I mourn in grey, grey as the sleeted
wind, the bled shades of twilight,
gunmetal, battleships, industrial paint,
the uniforms of trustees, the grey of proper
business suits and bankers' hearts,
the color of ash. Death comes in as fog.

Sun-day poacher

My Uncle Zimmy worked the face down in the soft
coal mines that hollowed out the long ridged
mountains of Pennsylvania, where the enamel
under the spigot in the claw tub at home
was stained the color of rust from iron.

In the winter he went down before the sun
came up, and when he rose, it had sunk,
a world of darkness down in the damp,
then up in the cold where the stars burned
like the sparks you see on squinted eyes.

On Sunday he hunted, gliding over the bristly
ridges that hid the tunnels, hollow rocks
whose blasted faces were bearded by shining ice.
That was his way to the sun blessing his eyes
and the tingling air the pines electrified.

He could only go with a rifle on his shoulder.
Men couldn't just walk and look. He had
to be doing something. With tenderness he sighted
the deer and shot true, disemboweled on the spot,
the snow marked with a widening rose of blood.

He butchered there and brought home venison,
better than the wan meat of the company store.
Nothing but bones would mark the spot in three
days. In winter, every bird and beast burns
with hunger, eats or snuffs out with cold.

He walked on top of the mountains he mined within
where and how he pleased, quiet as the snow
to kill. My aunt Margaret fell in love
with him and her father mocked and threatened.
A schoolteacher marry a miner? She did, fast.

You could see the way he touched her the power
they kindled between them. It was a dance
at Monday's Corners. He roared home on the icy
roads with the whiskey stoking that furnace hot.
That was how men drove: fast and often drunk.

He loved her still the year she lingered on.
Money could have saved her, of course.
A child, I ate his venison adoring him,
the strength and speed of a great black bear,
the same fatality in his embrace.

Northern lights of the skull

As I leaned over the book,
a snake coiled across my temples
dryly slithering
before slipping back into the earth.

I woke with fog clinging to me,
thickening, chilling the room air
blowing from that invisible ocean
that breaks always on our shore.

Time blows through my fissures
its slow magnetic storm,
fingers of ghostly auroral light
on which gusts of the dead

are borne like particles
of fine blinding ice
which turn the past day's light
into deep organ tones playing.

Time is the spooky dimension.
Would we book tickets to the past
like traveling to Dayton? Would we
summon ghosts like late night reruns?

Long burned hair brushes
across my face its spider
silk. I smell lavender,
cinnamon: my mother's clothes.

The terror lies, not
in the dead entering me
in icy probes of light,
in that chill that hollows the bones

but rather in how quickly
I blink my eyes clear
and rise, forgetting
as simply as fog burns off.

Burial by salt

The day after Thanksgiving I took you to the sea.
The sky was low and scudding. The wind was stiff.
The sea broke over itself in seething froth
like whipped up eggwhites, blowing to settle
in slowly popping masses at my feet.

I ran, boots on, into the bucking surf
taking you in handfuls, tossing you
into wind, into water, into the elements:
go back, give back. Time is all spent,
the flesh is spent to ashes.

Mother's were colored like a mosaic,
vivid hues of the inside of conch shells,
pastels, pearls, green, salmon as feathers
of tropical birds. They fit in my cupped hands.
I put her in the rose garden and said kaddish.

Your ashes are old movies, black into grey.
Heavy as iron filings, they sag the box
sides. They fill it to overflowing.
Handful after handful I give to the waves
which seize and churn you over and under.

I am silent as I give you to the cold
winter ocean grey as a ship of war,
the color of your eyes, grey with green
and blue washed in, that so seldom met
my gaze, that looked right through me.

What is to be said? Did you have a religion?
If so, you never spoke of it to me.

I remember you saying *No*, saying it often
and loud, I remember you saying, *Never*,
I remember, *I won't have that in my house.*

I grew up under the threat of your anger
as peasants occupy the slopes of a volcano
sniffing the wind, repeating old adages,
reading birdflight and always waiting, even
in sleep for the ground to quake and open.

My injustices, my pains, my resentments:
they are numerous, precious as the marbles
I kept in a jar, not so much for playing
as simply rolling in my hands to see
the colors trap the light and swell.

Tossing your ashes in my hands as the waves
drag the sand from under me, trying to topple
me into the turning eddy of far storms,
I want to cast that anger from me, finally,
to say, you begot me and although my body

my hair my eyes are my mother's so that at your
funeral, your brother called me by her name,
I will agree that in the long bones of my legs,
in my knees, in my Welsh mouth that sits oddly
in my Jewish Tartar face, you are imprinted.

I was born the wrong sex to a woman
in her mid-forties who had tried to get pregnant

for five years. A hard birth,
I was her miracle and your disappointment.
Everything followed from that, downhill.

I search now through the ashes of my old pain
to find something to praise, and I find that
withholding love, you made me strive to be worthy,
reaching, always reaching, thinking that when I leaped
high enough you would be watching. You weren't.

That did not cancel the leaping or the fruit
at last grasped in the hand and gnawed to the pit.
You were the stone on which I built my strength.
Your indifference honed me. Your coldness
toughened my flesh. Your anger stropped me.

I was reading maps for family trips at age
five, navigating from the back seat. Till
I was twenty, I did not know other children
did not direct all turns and plot route numbers.
When Mother feigned helplessness, I was factotum.

Nurse, houseboy, carpenter's helper, maid,
whatever chinks appeared I filled, responsible
and rebellious with equal passion, equal time,
and thus quite primed to charge like a rocket
out the door trailing sparks at seventeen.

We were illsuited as fox and bull. Once
I stopped following baseball, we could not talk.
I'd ask you how some process was done—open
hearth steel, how generators worked.
Your answers had a clarity I savored.

I did with mother as I had promised her,
I took her from you and brought her home to me,
I buried her as a Jew and mourn her still.
To you I made no promises. You asked none.
Forty-nine years we spoke of nothing real.

For decades I thought someday we would talk
at last. In California I came to you in the mountains
at the dam carrying that fantasy like a picnic
lunch beautifully cooked and packed, but never
to be eaten. Not by you and me.

When I think of the rare good times
I am ten or eleven and we are working together
on some task in silence. In silence I faded into
the cartoon son. Hand me the chisel. I handed.
Bevel the edge smooth. I always got bored.

I'd start asking questions, I'd start asking
why and wherefore and how come and who said so.
I was lonely on the icefield, I was lonely

in the ice caves of your sometime favor.
I kept trying to start a fire or conversation.

Time burns down and the dark rushes in in waves.
I can't lie. What was between us was history,
not love. I have striven to be just to you,
stranger, first cause, old man, my father,
and now I give you over to salt and silence.

A candle in a glass

When you died, it was time to light the first
candle of the eight. The dark tidal shifts
of the Jewish calendar of waters and the moon
that grows like a belly and starves like a rabbit
in winter have carried that holiday forward
and back since then. I light only your candle
at sunset, as the red wax of the sun melts
into the rumpled waters of the bay.

The ancient words pass like cold water
out of stone over my tongue as I say kaddish.
When I am silent and the twilight drifts
in on skeins of unraveling woolly snow
blowing over the hill dark with pitch pines,
I have a moment of missing that pierces
my brain like sugar stabbing a cavity
till the nerve lights its burning wire.

Grandmother Hannah comes to me at Pesach
and when I am lighting the sabbath candles.
The sweet wine in the cup has her breath.
The challah is braided like her long, long hair.
She smiles vaguely, nods, is gone like a savor
passing. You come oftener when I am putting

up pears or tomatoes, baking apple cake.
You are in my throat laughing or in my eyes.

When someone dies, it is the unspoken words
that spoil in the mind and ferment to wine
and to vinegar. I obey you still, going
out in the saw toothed wind to feed the birds
you protected. When I lie in the arms of my love,
I know how you climbed like a peavine twining,
lush, grasping for the sun, toward love
and always you were pinched back, denied.

It's a little low light the yahrzeit candle
makes, you couldn't read by it or even warm
your hands. So the dead are with us only
as the scent of fresh coffee, of cinnamon,
of pansies excites the nose and then fades,
with us as the small candle burns in its glass.
We lose and we go on losing as long as we live,
a little winter no spring can melt.

THE RAM'S HORN

Le Sacre du Printemps

1. The Great Serpent Mound, Ohio

Seven great sensuous coils project
themselves forward across the plateau in motion
caught—not frozen—as if poised.

Toward the tail, the snake curls itself
round and round and round seven times
to the tiny center of an exclamation point

like a cat turning and turning in place
till she lies down to sleep, a ritual
whose significance causes her to smile.

The head end is open and striking.
Violence as dance, dance as sculpture.
Spiral coiling as a vine climbs a tree.

Does the serpent bite the sun?
Does she sink her teeth into the moon?
Is it her egg she carries in her mouth?

She invokes a dance too long awaited,
for she is as fearsome as she is playful,
and the tail still sleeps while the head strikes.

2. Grotte de Font–de–Gaume, Périgord

How sexual they are, the snorting bison,
the male and female poised to court,
their delicate rear legs, their massive heads

lowered or raised sniffing, eyes wide.
The artist crawled through the stone cervix
and here raised her smoky lamp to draw

deep in the hills' womb, herself half
dissolved in the darkness, courting terror,
working with a hand that never shook,

sure in its lines as if it drew a bow
before a charging bison. No one with eyes
could call these paintings crude.

The mastery is double, art and the observed
animal, exactly how the male would paw,
how the female would turn her head and blow,

how the deer would leap a log in headlong
flight, how the haunches bunch and knot.
Immensely knowing she was : love looks so.

And love does bite into that sweet flesh.
Passion binds the predator to prey,
the arrows of desire driving for the heart.

The light and the green blood that the bison
stole from the grass, she will pluck
from his haunch, if her hand is quick enough.

3. The garden as synagogue

Some of my best friends are vegetarians.
With sorrow they consider me. My eating of flesh
appears to them a weakness of character

like a fine humanitarian who pays callgirls
to piss in his ear. I feed the sparrows,
but when the hawk stoops at them, I welcome her.

She comes, wings outspread and then folding
slightly as she drops to the carcass or lure,
hawkheaded winged falconwoman with steel talons.

Totem lady looming out of the fog, ancient
witness of a joining we fail, except with pets,
the last animals we touch beyond our mangled

selves, so that all we will ever know of wildness
is contained in the cat's leap, the dog's
lunge, the skittish hooves of the overbred horse.

Yet I dream you again and again, goddess
rooted in animal power and grace, the sacred
that connects us to the green flesh

of the grass, the green blood of the tree,
the cool slow rippling world of the fish
and the hot fast beady passions of the bird.

We have dropped so far from the nipple of the earth
we think the cow is more alive than the oak tree;
we imagine the soil is inert as plastic flooring;

we forget to thank our food and we play with it
as if it were a deck of cards; and we will use
only the nines and sevens and pass by the queens.

Our minds float on the waters that flow
through the limestone rock, through the jewelweed,
through the tadpole, blood of the earth

circling. The copper, the iron that will color
your ashes have looked out through the walleye
of the pike and stained the peacock's tail.

The hawk is as good a hawk as the sparrow
is sparrow, simmering in the stone soup
that death stirs. Death shadows all body

whether of sequoia or snail, grasshopper
or whale, cod or cabbage plant, lily
or lotus, we are one great dispersed flesh.

At the seder I eat the lamb, the egg, the bitter
herbs, the apples and almonds and I am healed
to the sprouting earth that bears them all in me.

I feel myself suspended fighting, using the winds
of history, riding the updraft, plunging
through the downdraft, the fierce winds sucking

my bones light and thin till they cast me down.
A poet told me a plane starts aging fast the moment
it takes off and all the time it is held aloft.

I come to earth, I come back to soil, I kneel.
You are history rich and crumbling in my hand.
I am of you and soon shall be in you. Amen.

Moves on the ceiling

In the dark all things become
what we secretly suspect them to be:
the car bares its toothy grille and springs;
the footboard knobs huddle like owls watching
for the quaking mouse to break cover and run;
the tree casts a net of bony clutching fingers;
the open door is a mast topped by a skull.

In childhood, did I ever sleep?
The feverish huddle of nights spent
watching the blinds watch me.
What did I fear so fervidly?
People kept dying then of accidents,
of cancer, of the war, but my parents'
war had wounded the only civilian, me.

The night turns us out like pockets
bottomed with forlorn forgotten garbage,
the broken pencils and enigmatic
torn scraps of fear, the irreducible
detritus of tedious nightmare,
the unpaid bills gathering monstrous
interest, dusty summonses.

As we thrash in that dark warm sea
of the blood under the angling moon,
something brushes our dangling legs.
Everything we have dismissed
but not defeated circles up to feed
on us as the tidy membranes of ego
tear and the self shreds on those teeth.

What do we fear most in the dark?
To encounter the alien, the grim
implacable and hungry tiger for whom
no word of pleading is more than the grunt
of food making ready? Or to look into the tiger's
eye and read our own knowledge of how sweet
and how salty is fresh blood.

How divine is forgiving?

It's a nice concept
but what's under the sculptured draperies?
We forgive when we don't really care
because what was done to us brought unexpected
harvest, as I always try to explain
to the peach trees as I prune them hard,
to the cats when I shove pills against
the Gothic vaults of their mouths.

We forgive those who betrayed us
years later because memory has rotted
through like something left out in the weather
battered clean then littered dirty
in the rain, chewed by mice and beetles,
frozen and baked and stripped by the wind
till it is unrecognizable, corpse
or broken machine, something long useless.

We forgive those whom their own machinations
have sufficiently tangled, enshrouded,
the fly who bit us to draw blood and who
hangs now a gutted trophy in a spider's
airy larder; more exactly, the friend
whose habit of lying has immobilized him
at last like a dog trapped in a cocoon
of fishing line and barbed hooks.

We forgive those we firmly love
because anger hurts, a coal that burns
and smoulders still scorching the tissues
inside, blistering wherever it touches
so that finally it is to ease our own pain
that we bury the hot clinkers in a mound
of caring, suffocate the sparks with promises,
drown them in tears, reconciling.

We forgive mostly not from strength
but through imperfections, for memory
wears transparent as a glass with the pattern
washed off, till we stare past what injured us.
We forgive because we too have done
the same to others easy as a mudslide;
or because anger is a fire that must be fed
and we are too tired to rise and haul a log.

The New Year of the Trees

It is the New Year of the Trees, but here
the ground is frozen under the crust of snow.
The trees snooze, their buds tight as nuts.
Rhododendron leaves roll up their stiff scrolls.

In the white and green north of the diaspora
I am stirred by a season that will not arrive
for six weeks, as wines on far continents prickle
to bubbles when their native vines bloom.

What blossoms here are birds jostling
at feeders, pecking sunflower seeds
and millet through the snow: tulip red
cardinal, daffodil finch, larkspur jay,

the pansybed of sparrows and juncos, all hungry.
They too are planters of trees, spreading seeds
of favorites along fences. On the earth closed
to us all as a book in a language we cannot

yet read, the seeds, the bulbs, the eggs
of the fervid green year await release.
Over them on February's cold table I spread
a feast. Wings rustle like summer leaves.

Summer mourning

One summer morning the light pools heavy
with exhaust fumes on the dying grass;
every leaf on every tree bears the marks
of gnawing, of the teeth of caterpillars,
or is soiled with brown rot or fuzzy mold;
in dawn's yellow rose, the Japanese beetle
has chewed and shat and now couples in bronze.
There is a time when summer rusts like wheat.

In the fullness of the melon moon the void
of new moon coils like a seed; in the ripeness
of harvest we mourn failure and almost-beens.
Tishah b'Av. With the feast comes mourning
for as the year slides down from its fiery peak
the spiral of other summers and other years
unwinds ghostly behind. Sometimes the heat
and the humidity feel like inertia

and I struggle against history as a fly
caught on flypaper: swimming in molasses.
Sometimes history seems to me the bad air
in a tunnel where I am trapped in rush hour
traffic, all these cars at one time stalled
pumping out poison, one angry person in each
drumming their fingers on the steering wheel
and longing for teleportation.

How many marriages choke on their own debris,
the habits of old anger, an arthritis

disabling motion. Ancient injustices
still leak their poison into the water table
while new ones irradiate the skulls of embryos.
Tishah b'Av. I know how the cost of change
cuts down to the living bone; and how the cost
of what is, is the bone rotting from within.

Perfect weather

On the six o'clock news, Ken poses in his three
piece blue suit in front of the map of fronts.
Barbie pretends to slap at him. "Now Ken,
I hope you aren't going to give us bad weather!"
"I'm giving you perfect 10 weather, Barbie,
not a cloud all weekend! Not a storm in sight
on our Super Weather Radar. Another
perfect week coming up." "Oh, thank you, Ken!"

Gods in the box, they pop out grinning.
Next will come the announcements of water
shortages on the South Shore, crop
failure in the Pioneer Valley, a fire raging
through the pitch pines near Sandwich.
Turn on the faucet, Barbie. Think that's
manufactured in some plant in Maine?
Shipped from Taiwan like your microphone?

It arrives in pellets called rain drops. That's
what you call bad and mean it: nasty weather.
They want a permanent pasted on sun
to shine over the freeze dried face and the body
resembling exactly a mannequin in a shop
window sipping an empty glass on Astroturf.
That body will never thicken or that face
admit it liked to smile or frown: wiped memory.

A permanent now called lobotomy
under a sunlamp sky, a neon moon, life as a golf
course unrolled from a truck and every day
you can play. Everyone you meet has just

your skin color and income level; the dis-
functional are removed immediately to storage.
Service personnel speak another language.
Death comes as a power failure.

Ken, how's supper? Did you know bluefish
swim? Kiwi grow on trees made of bad weather
juice? Perrier actually bubbles out of rock?
Under the carpet under the cracking cement
below the power lines and the toxic waste stored
in old mines is molten rock, the hot liquid heart
of the earth beating, about to erupt
blowing the clots out of its ancient veins.

We don't own the earth, not even the way
you buy a condo, Ken. We don't time-share
here, but live on it as hair grows
on the scalp, from inside; we are part
of earth, not visitors using the facilities.
If the plumbing breaks down, we can't move out
to a bigger house. Rain is earth's blood
and ours while we swim and life swims in us.

Pray for rain. Go out on the earth barefoot
and dance for rain. Take a small
ceremonial knife and slash your arms
so the thick red water inside trickles out.
Piss in the dust. Spit into the wind.
Go climb a mountain without a canteen to learn
how the swollen tongue sticks to the palate.
Then tell us what good weather you're providing.

Wellfleet sabbath

The hawk eye of the sun slowly shuts.
The breast of the bay is softly feathered
dove grey. The sky is barred like the sand
when the tide trickles out.

The great doors of the sabbath are swinging
open over the ocean, loosing the moon
floating up slow   distorted   vast, a copper
balloon just sailing free.

The wind slides over the waves, patting
them with its giant hand, and the sea
stretches its muscles in the deep,
purrs and rolls over.

The sweet beeswax candles flicker
and sigh, standing between the phlox
and the roast chicken. The wine shines
its red lantern of joy.

Here on this piney sandspit, the Shekinah
comes on the short strong wings of the seaside
sparrow raising her song and bringing
down the fresh clean night.

I saw her dancing

1.

Because I saw her change
Because I saw her
            change
Cuba in the simmering summer of sixty-eight
when the walls of the ghettoed world seemed to be melting
from the heat of our bodies and our blazing minds
into wax dripping down a wine bottle
and the sun itself was the bright candle.

Santos, santaría
Drum speaking to drum
each a heart pounding   each a womb throbbing
hands caressing, teasing, spanking, kneading the stretched
      skin.

An old woman was dancing to the drums, in faded cotton
      skirts
scrawny chicken neck, loose shuddering arms
washerwoman toeing and swirling to the rhythms
when Yemanja came to ride her.

My knees jellied. My eyes burned of smoke.
Then I was turning in place, a top
whirled by a string,
for her face sparkled like a waterfall in sunlight
for her skin was smooth as still water
that plays mirror to the moon's leaning face
for her arms were lithe and snapping snakes

118

for she swayed tall as a coconut palm
her hips rolled to the waves calling them home
and teasing them out again
    and she changed
    and she changed
    and she changed
and seeing I was shaken like water troubled to the bottom
stones the water punishes and polishes bright.

Then it was again an old woman
flabby and limp and washed out like old cotton shirts
pounded on the rocks and bleached in the sun
too many times and hard years.

2.

Because all poets know how the god
seizes you by the nape and shakes till your bones
vibrate all their tuning forks on key
taking you from behind like a great tomcat
mounting you with teeth gripped in your skin
pulling tight, tight as a drum.

Because all artists know the self
is a bag of roaring winds northeast, south, west
coiling for a curious fool to loose them,
and all artists are fools who push on and in
servants of chaos and of order in each season
as Persephone labored to please death and fertility

finding in herself both seed and skull
the flower that opens at each end of life.

Because all women know being used
by what wants to come into the world, by what scratches
and claws and gouges its way toward light,
and then starts screaming its lungs sore,
needing infinite labor just to keep in the air.

3.

I a Jew saw Yemanja and worshiped
as I have met other goddesses
in dark and shining places.

It is all many as fingers and toes and the hair of your head
and it is all one.
It is all one as an egg, as a seed, as stone, as a fire
and it is all many.

I know I know I know   I am known
in silence liquid and dark as oil
still locked in rock, in the hot peristaltic bowels of earth.

Yanking my hair hard till my eyes tear,
she touches the nape there
breathing out her fiery dragon's breath
and I am changed.

We are lit up and then the light fades out.
I stand in the field pelted with the rain
and wait for the forked gift to electrify me.

Nothing living moves in straight lines
but in arcs, in epicycles, in spirals, in gyres.
Nothing living grows in cubes or cones or rhomboids
but we take a little here and give a little here
and we change
and the wind blows right through us and knocks the apples
from the tree and hangs a red kite suddenly there
and a fox comes to bite the apples curiously
and we change
or die
and then change.
It is many as drops
it is one as rain
and we are in it, in it, of it.
We eat it and it eats us
and fullness is never and now.

Nishmat

When the night slides under with the last dimming star
and the red sky lightens between the trees,
and the heron glides tipping heavy wings in the river,
when crows stir and cry out their harsh joy,
and swift creatures of the night run toward their burrows,
and the deer raises her head and sniffs the freshening air,
and the shadows grow more distinct and then shorten,

then we rise into the day still clean as new snow.
The cat washes its paw and greets the day with gratitude.
Leviathan salutes breaching with a column of steam.
The hawk turning in the sky cries out a prayer like a knife.
We must wonder at the sky now thin as a speckled eggshell,
that now piles up its boulders of storm to crash down,
that now hangs a furry grey belly into the street.

Every day we find a new sky and a new earth
with which we are trusted like a perfect toy.
We are given the salty river of our blood
winding through us, to remember the sea and our
kindred under the waves, the hot pulsing that knocks
in our throats to consider our cousins in the grass
and the trees, all bright scattered rivulets of life.

We are given the wind within us, the breath
to shape into words that steal time, that touch
like hands and pierce like bullets, that waken
truth and deceit, sorrow and pity and joy,
that waste precious air in complaints, in lies,
in floating traps for power on the dirty air.
Yet holy breath still stretches our lungs to sing.

122

We are given the body, that momentary kibbutz
of elements that have belonged to frog and polar
bear, corn and oak tree, volcano and glacier.
We are lent for a time these minerals in water
and a morning every day, a morning to wake up,
rejoice and praise life in our spines, our throats,
our knees, our genitals, our brains, our tongues.

We are given fire to see against the dark,
to think, to read, to study how we are to live,
to bank in ourselves against defeat and despair
that cool and muddy our resolves, that make us forget
what we saw we must do. We are given passion
to rise like the sun in our minds with the new day
and burn the debris of habit and greed and fear.

We stand in the midst of the burning world
primed to burn with compassionate love and justice,
to turn inward and find holy fire at the core,
to turn outward and see the world that is all
of one flesh with us, see under the trash, through
the smog, the furry bee in the apple blossom,
the trout leaping, the candles our ancestors lit for us.

Fill us as the tide rustles into the reeds in the marsh.
Fill us as the rushing water overflows the pitcher.
Fill us as light fills a room with its dancing.
Let the little quarrels of the bones and the snarling
of the lesser appetites and the whining of the ego cease.
Let silence still us so you may show us your shining
and we can out of that stillness rise and praise.

Maggid

The courage to let go of the door, the handle.
The courage to shed the familiar walls whose very
stains and leaks are comfortable as the little moles
of the upper arm; stains that recall a feast,
a child's naughtiness, a loud blattering storm
that slapped the roof hard, pouring through.

The courage to abandon the graves dug into the hill,
the small bones of children and the brittle bones
of the old whose marrow hunger had stolen;
the courage to desert the tree planted and only
begun to bear; the riverside where promises were
shaped; the street where their empty pots were broken.

The courage to leave the place whose language you learned
as early as your own, whose customs however dan-
gerous or demeaning, bind you like a halter
you have learned to pull inside, to move your load;
the land fertile with the blood spilled on it;
the roads mapped and annotated for survival.

The courage to walk out of the pain that is known
into the pain that cannot be imagined,
mapless, walking into the wilderness, going
barefoot with a canteen into the desert;
stuffed in the stinking hold of a rotting ship
sailing off the map into dragons' mouths,

Cathay, India, Siberia, goldeneh medina,
leaving bodies by the way like abandoned treasure.
So they walked out of Egypt. So they bribed their way
out of Russia under loads of straw; so they steamed
out of the bloody smoking charnelhouse of Europe
on overloaded freighters forbidden all ports—

out of pain into death or freedom or a different
painful dignity, into squalor and politics.
We Jews are all born of wanderers, with shoes
under our pillows and a memory of blood that is ours
raining down. We honor only those Jews who changed
tonight, those who chose the desert over bondage,

who walked into the strange and became strangers
and gave birth to children who could look down
on them standing on their shoulders for having
been slaves. We honor those who let go of every-
thing but freedom, who ran, who revolted, who fought,
who became other by saving themselves.

The ram's horn sounding

1.

Giant porcupine, I walk a rope braided
of my intestines and veins, beige and blue and red,
while clutched in my arms, you lie glaring
sore eyed, snuffling and sticking your spines at me.

Always I am finding quills worked into some unsuspected
muscle, an innocent pillow of fat pierced by you.
We sleep in the same bed nightly and you take it all.
I wake shuddering with cold, the quilt stripped from me.

No, not a porcupine: a leopard cub.
Beautiful you are as light and as darkness.
Avid, fierce, demanding with sharp teeth
to be fed and tended, you only want my life.

Ancient, living, a deep and tortuous river
that rose in the stark mountains beyond the desert,
you have gouged through rocks with slow persistence
enduring, meandering in long shining coils to the sea.

2.

A friend who had been close before being recruited
by the CIA once sent me a postcard of the ghetto at Tetuàn
yellowed like old pornography numbered 17,
a prime number as one might say a prime suspect.

126

The photographer stood well clear of the gate
to shoot old clothes tottering in the tight street,
beards matted and holy with grease,
children crooked under water jugs,
old men austere and busy as hornets.
Flies swarmed on the lens.
Dirt was the color.

Oh, I understood your challenge.
My Jewishness seemed to you sentimental,
perverse, planned obsolescence.
Paris was hot and dirty the night I first
met relatives who had survived the war.
My identity squatted whining on my arm
gorging itself on my thin blood.
A gaggle of fierce insistent speakers of ten
languages had different passports mother
from son, brother from sister, had four
passports all forged, kept passports
from gone countries (Transylvania, Bohemia,
old despotisms fading like Victorian wallpaper),
were used to sewing contraband into coat
linings. I smuggled for them across two borders.
Their wars were old ones.
Mine was just starting.

Old debater, it's easy in any manscape
to tell the haves from the have-nots.
Any ghetto is a kleinbottle.

You think you are outside gazing idly in.
Winners write history; losers
die of it, like the plague.

3.

A woman and a Jew, sometimes more
of a contradiction than I can sweat out,
yet finally the intersection that is both
collision and fusion, stone and seed.

Like any poet I wrestle the holy name
and know there is no wording finally
can map, constrain or summon that fierce
voice whose long wind lifts my hair

chills my skin and fills my lungs
to bursting. I serve the word
I cannot name, who names me daily,
who speaks me out by whispers and shouts.

Coming to the new year, I am picked
up like the ancient ram's horn to sound
over the congregation of people and beetles,
of pines, whales, marshhawks and asters.

Then I am dropped into the factory of words
to turn my little wheels and grind my own

edges, back on piece work again, knowing
there is no justice we don't make daily

like bread and love. Shekinah,
stooping on hawk wings prying into my heart
with your silver beak; floating down
a milkweed silk dove of sunset;

riding the filmy sheets of rain like a ghost
ship with all sails still unfurled;
bless me and use me for telling and naming
the forever collapsing shades and shapes of life,

the rainbows cast across our eyes by the moment
of sun, the shadows we trail across the grass
running, the opal valleys of the night flesh,
the moments of knowledge ripping into the brain

and aligning everything into a new pattern
as a constellation learned organizes blur
into stars, the blood kinship with all green, hairy
and scaled folk born from the ancient warm sea.

A note about the author

Marge Piercy is the author of ten books of poetry: *Breaking Camp, Hard Loving, 4-Telling, To Be of Use, Living in the Open, The Twelve-Spoked Wheel Flashing, The Moon Is Always Female, Circles on the Water: Selected Poems, Stone, Paper, Knife* and *My Mother's Body*. She has also published nine novels: *Going Down Fast, Dance the Eagle to Sleep, Small Changes, Woman on the Edge of Time, The High Cost of Living, Vida, Braided Lives, Fly Away Home* and *Gone to Soldiers*. The University of Michigan Press published a volume of her essays, reviews and interviews, entitled *Parti-Colored Blocks for a Quilt*, as part of their Poets on Poetry Series. She has also co-authored a play, *The Last White Class*, with her husband, Ira Wood, and edited an anthology entitled *Early Ripening: American Women's Poetry Now*. She and her husband live in Wellfleet, Massachusetts.

A note on the type

This book was set on the Linotype in Century Expanded, designed in 1894 by Linn Boyd Benton (1844–1932). Benton cut Century Expanded in response to Theodore De Vinne's request for an attractive, easy-to-read typeface to fit the narrow columns of his *Century Magazine*. Early in the nineteen hundreds Morris Fuller Benton updated and improved Century in several versions for his father's American Type Founders Company. Century remains the only American typeface cut before 1910 still widely in use today.

Composed by Maryland Linotype Composition Company, Baltimore, Maryland. Printed and bound by The Haddon Craftsmen, Inc., Scranton, Pennsylvania. Typography and binding design by Virginia Tan.